By Way of Introduction

BY WAY OF INTRODUCTION

STEVE WESTBY

Copyright © 2022 Steve Westby
stevewestby@yahoo.com

ISBN 979-8-218-00492-7

Edited and designed by Tell Tell Poetry

Printed in the United States of America

First Printing, 2022

To all my fellow sparks

Contents

Poem for a Friend   3

Healing
Gravity   7
Recall how you feel when someone you love enters the room.   8
Human Being   9
Four Ties   10
Zoloft   11
I read today that everything done in love is healing work.   12

Worth
Self   15
I used to think   16
Genesis   17
Don't read this poem   18
We don't just talk; we sing.   19
Wakening   20
If we could see beyond the fireworks of doing   21
when Self is hidden   22

Seasons
217   25
Hospice   26
My mom passed away today.   27
Autumn   28
Lent   29
Mental Health Day   30
advent   31
wisdom is elusive to the mind   32
Garden   33

Love

Bathe your heart   37

Holy   38

Hubris   39

Walking Protest   40

Repair   41

Compassion

Pause   45

Peace Treaty   46

Last Laugh   47

we imagine   48

Batman   49

Breath   50

perhaps on your journey   51

Acknowledgments:

I would like to acknowledge all of those who have provided input, support, and encouragement in putting this book together.

Thank you to my fiancée, Nicole, and to my sons, Patrick and Jacob.

Thanks to my friend, Cathi, who kindly provided guidance on my initial collection of poems and whose input I relied upon for organization and clarity.

Thanks to my good friends, Pat and John, for believing in the worth of my poems and encouraging me to put these out into the world.

Thanks to everyone I have met on my IFS journey, for opening their hearts and offering their wisdom.

And finally, thanks to the amazing team of people at Tell Tell Poetry, whose support, expertise, and input has been invaluable.

I offer my deepest gratitude to all of you.

By Way of Introduction

Poem for a Friend

If this finds you in soul's dark night
Where cares make weary
Day's long plight

I ask but this:
When darkness falls
Call that I might be
A willing firefly

Sputtering, yes
Not so bright, mayhap
But yours

Healing

Gravity

I expected drama
A blinding inner light
A sudden "aha!"
Or the embodied, cathartic defeat
Of some inner demon, howling
Its defiant rage

Healing is none of these
Not a confrontation, but an openness
Not a battle, but the slow steady
Courage of curiosity

It's a moment when understanding deepens
Compassion seeps through our walls like water
Settling into cracks and pores, guided silently
Into the soul's depths
Gravity's bend inexorably pulling

Until nothing has changed. And everything undone.

Recall how you feel when someone you love enters the room.

Think of that joy—not because they've done something but because they exist.

Now consider that that same feeling happens all the time. About you. In the hearts of those who love you.

Sit with that, if just for thirty seconds. Let that feeling settle into your soul. Notice any shifts as you allow this into your heart.

If you find this healing, I invite you to share the joy you experience with your friends, your spouse, your children. Express it openly, sincerely, gladly. Let this be your gift to them.

Human Being

Starlight made dense
Love calcified in fear
Yearning for its source

Four Ties

I could show you a map
Oh, and tell stories
Of demons and wisdom and grace

But I would wish for you instead
A beginning step
On a journey of wondrous discovery

And a pen to mark its passage

Zoloft

An SSRI can glue the soul
Calming an inner war
So the world slows down
And fear gives up its throne

No medicine, though, can keep out the rain
Offering little solace
When torrents of loneliness or pain
Pummel the heart

Sometimes savior
Sometimes not

Joy demands more
Than sertraline's wisdom

I read today that everything done in love is healing work.

I agree with the sentiment. I also find it incomplete.

If I were permitted to elaborate, I might say that love is a requirement for any act to be healing. But to heal, we must also bring our wisdom.

We need to deeply understand the person and issue we are trying to heal, lest our love miss the mark. (We might tell our children repeatedly of our love for them, but that is unlikely to bring healing when we are blind to the nature of their pain.)

We must also bring our courage on the healing journey. We need to listen, to sit with feelings and truths we might rather avoid.

Only wise, courageous love can be extended to areas of the soul we have locked away. This is particularly important when we seek to heal ourselves.

Worth

Self

your parents saw it when you were born, saw within you

the flame of long dead stars, and held you close because

your spark is infinitely precious

you might have glimpsed it when you were five and danced

furiously in the rain for the pure joy of movement

when you loved with all your heart

when your heart was broken and you rose to love again

when laughter overcame all pretense

when you stopped singing and simply became the song

life's great joy is that this

is you

and the rest of us are just so glad you are here

I used to think

I couldn't dance
Until I realized
We are always dancing

Some skillfully
Others less so
But that matters little—

We sway
To an inner song

The steps are choreographed
The moves mechanical and plodding
Like square dancing in seventh grade
To music mournful and slow
Returning, always, to where you began

Healing is a new dance
Music that pulls your heart and limbs
Gracelessly, perhaps
Yet there you are

Dancing and alive
Your heart discovers it can choose the steps

Your teen may protest their embarrassment
But music, rhythm, and uncoordinated feet
Move you across the floor

Genesis

God's first touch
Sent the stuff of stars
Hurtling trillions of miles

Formed the mountains
Gave life to the oceans
And ultimately formed you

Do not doubt
That you can heal
Or grow or become more

Your essence is the stuff of stars
And God's impertinent mischief

Don't read this poem

If this verse is mere words
You shouldn't waste your time

Find instead the stuff of life
Oh, you will know its embrace
Which will charge the marrow
Of your bones

Find those moments
When love springs to your lips
Like laughter from children

When joy bubbles up
Unbounded and pure

Drink deeply
Let this be your sustenance
And live

We don't just talk; we sing.

We focus so much on words that we forget we are singing.

Fail to notice if the song is soft or harsh, measured or rapid, loving or disdainful.

We forget what we know to be true: that music conveys love and acceptance and belonging in ways words alone could not.

Forget what your fifth-grade music teacher told you about whether you can hold a tune.

Know instead that every utterance you make is song.

Choose chords of love and joy, belonging and remembrance, to fill the night sky of each other's souls.

Wakening

What is it that we see?

If you stand before my fear of rejection, will I see you?

Will I notice the gentle laughter in your smile?

If my mind is beset by self-loathing, can my soul

accept the warmth in your eyes?

If my heart is raging, could I possibly sense the vulnerable

wound that led to a careless remark?

But if not, have I seen you?

Do my walls shield me more from life than from harm?

If I missed your laughter, warmth, or woundedness,

have I not failed to see what is essential?

Have I stepped back from life, acting out a play written long ago—

a lonely tragedy with an ending I already know too well?

Opening my eyes reveals joy in the present, yes.

But also what was missed.

A wake for joy unrealized.

If we could see beyond the fireworks of doing

Hush for a moment the flash bangs of thought
Perhaps we might notice
The soft warm light of our being
Suffusing the world with joy

when Self is hidden

call her name

if you've forgotten
search your memory

you may find her
giggling in joy
as you greeted a friend

or pouring her heart out
when your daughter skinned a knee

yearning to help the world
in the face of darkness

or in awe
of sunset's beauty

she is this echo
of eternity
waiting to be remembered

lean in—

perhaps she will whisper
her secrets
in a tongue lost to despair

but found
again and again
in the laugh of a child

Seasons

217

She lay silent
Posed in the hospital bed
And I touched her arm
Thinking she might
Sense comfort
Or maybe I hoped
To feel life
To recall moments
When her touch
Reassured
One last time
Before mortality's jealous grasp
Robbed me of her warmth

Hospice

Are you leaving
Have you gone

When I touch your face
Do you recall
The hugs
The laughs
The fights

Has the injury stolen your soul
Or does some part still linger

Recognizing us
Or wishing
For your favorite ice cream
Or voices of your beloved

Can you hear my plaintive cry

Or are you beyond

Looking down and wishing
Your flesh could respond

To grasp our hands
Murmur that you hear us

And whisper your goodbye

My mom passed away today.

I'm not quite sure how to form the words to make that make sense.

My mom's story could be told in simple terms. I could tell you she was born in Detroit, raised (mostly) in California, married my dad ten days after she turned eighteen, and had six kids.

I could tell you how she dove headfirst into Girl Scouts, how our basement was full of Thin Mints and Samoas and Tagalong cookies each year, or how she always had to order more because we'd sneak down into the basement and eat our favorites.

I could tell you about how fiercely she loved her grandchildren, how much she doted on them and found joy in them. Or I could tell you of her fury and the force of her personality when our defiance met her ire.

I could tell you of her pain and sacrifice, caring for my father as he slowly declined until Pick's disease claimed his life in 2005.

I could tell you how she ran a daycare out of our home and how she helped shape the lives of numerous kids.

I could tell you how I loved her or how we used to butt heads as I became an adolescent—and how all these feelings morphed as she and I both grew over time.

Now none of that can capture her spark, her fire, or what she meant to me. I think I will just say that I loved her, and I miss her. Maybe in time I will find better words.

Or maybe this is one of those things words cannot capture.

Goodbye, Mom. May you rest in peace.

Autumn

Let rest a moment
The bright green splash of leaves
Or dazzling red and yellow flowers

See instead the structure
The earth sharing its nutrients
The tree extending its branches

Patient, waiting
Offering life to the world

Lent

We give up the wrong things

Eliminating candy instead of self-criticism
Sex instead of selfishness

Acting as if what God desires most
Is for us to be on a diet from joy

Perhaps Lent should instead
Be a time of letting go
Of all that prevents community

Mental Health Day

Perhaps today
Sing a love song
To all within
That sits in darkness

Share their yoke
Mop their brow
Listen and hear

Mayhap gentle touch
Might pierce isolation
For the briefest of moments

And hope
A bud in spring
Pokes through pain's soil
To seek the light

advent

radar pings of worry
shadow
a peace, a love
so vast
it suffuses the universe

let me gather, then
this child in my arms
hold and comfort them

until in safety they rest
and joy is born

wisdom is elusive to the mind

we are fools if we try
and fools if we don't

fools if we break our hearts (or theirs)
and fools if we never risk a breaking

fools if success makes us haughty
fools if fear prevents risk

we might despair
worshiping at worry's throne

but my grandmother would laugh
with eyes that journeyed a million lifetimes

Garden

If heaven had Twitter,
I imagine our beloved
Might remind us how our being
Brought joy to their hearts,
Direction when lost—
Warmth to winter's chill.

Then they might slyly confess:
"These I have sown in the earth of your soul,
That my memory might grow flowers."

Love

Bathe your heart

In the joy of children

Let their bright eyes
And exuberant souls
Soak into your marrow

So you might offer
A softened heart
Overflowing
With love and delight

To a world
Aching in loneliness

Holy

They say
Matter
Is energy slowed down.

They say
Personality
Is just mind
Regulating energy's flow.

But what if
This energy
Behind and amidst all things
Is love?

What if the mystics sing true:
That grace pervades,
Our hearts are sacred,
And sin a kind of blindness?

We might wake up,
Behold our greatest fears,
And laugh with joy.

Hubris

Cold slowly devouring
Warmth from my cheeks
Forcing my body to match
Its ferocity or perish

Or perhaps to flee
To run and shelter
Far from season's wrath

But the spell is broken
By joy on my son's face
Invigorated by the chill

Walking Protest

I think today
I will love more fiercely
My fellow humans

Be they POC or white
LGBTQIA or straight
From this country or not

I will love them
Because they are

And let that love
Silence my lips

When empty words
Are blasphemy

Repair

I thought I was paying for armor
A knowledge I could gird into battle
Or a sword—oh, how I would have
Loved a sword to slay the beast
That threatened my certainty

I was so wrong
Seeking armor, I witnessed instead
A thousand brilliant stars

Courageous open hearts
Baring tender injury
And somehow releasing love

Seeking a sword, I found instead
A million warm smiles

Greeting near strangers
Until shared laughs and pain
Build the miracle of friendship

I came seeking armor
Or a part of me did

But how could I have known
The true gift would be you
My dear friends

Opening my eyes to see
New light
Born of your witness

Compassion

Pause

Cease for a moment
Your thinking and doing

Turn your ear inside
Listen to the cries of your heart

Let each feeling know you are there
Listening, hearing

Set aside the outside world
Sow compassion in your soul

Peace Treaty

Today curiosity bade me notice
A battle waging
Between self-hate and avoidance

Yet I found I could honor
Self-hate for its unending labor
To prevent me from failing

Avoidance
For its desperate vigil
To stave off rejection

Seeing their hearts anew
Compassion stopped labeling them as enemy
And declared peace in my soul

Last Laugh

My grand plan fails
Felled by reality
And self-importance

Laughter bubbles up
On its own
Wisdom's mirth irrepressibly born

we imagine

that we are simple
that we just do things

like drive
or talk
or work
or jog

our simple attention
neglects the chorus
singing to the world
our greatest fear

we work amidst a wail of mourning
parent lyrics of frustration
sit quietly in a dirge of unending heartbreak

listen instead
to the music
add your voice to its refrain

join in the song

see if you might add

a simple note

of joy

Batman

When we were young,
My family traveled
A thousand miles
To see you, my cousin.

Our play stretched for hours.
You were Batman
And I a bystander.

Your brilliance
Sparked a thousand games,
A thousand days' memories
Haunting me still.

How did I fail to see the darkness
Was self-destruction
Casually hidden?

Were you blind to being my hero?
Or did your genius obscure
A hero's heart
As desperation grew—

Batman shockingly cancelled
At the point of a barrel
Near the loveliness of a stream.

Breath

Today
A young girl
In sunlight
Allowed me witness
Pain and fury,
Trauma, deep and raw,
Spanning years.

I saw a true hero
Open her heart—
Hear her,
Sit with her,
Protect her.

Until the girl,
Safe and loved,

Breathed away
Shame—
A moral reckoning
That was never her own.

perhaps on your journey

you will come across
a pool of infinite sorrow

jump in if you'd like
let childlike joy
send unexpected waves
across its surface

or wade in reverently
gently touching its depths

let the coolness feel your warmth

and don't worry

you will discover

your heart is bigger

www.ingramcontent.com/pod-product-compliance
Lightning Source LLC
LaVergne TN
LVHW041204080426
835511LV00006B/731